# July

K. C. KELLEY • BOB OSTROM

**The Child's World**

Published by The Child's World®
1980 Lookout Drive • Mankato, MN  56003-1705
800-599-READ • www.childsworld.com

Acknowledgments
The Child's World®: Mary Berendes, Publishing Director
The Design Lab: Design
Jody Jensen Shaffer: Editing and Fact-Checking

Photo credits
© Alexius Sutandio/Shutterstock.com: 11 (bottom); amelaxa/
Shutterstock.com: 12 (bottom); antares71/iStock.com: cover, 1, 5;
Fer Gregory/Shutterstock.com: 11 (top); Gamutstockimagespvtltd/
Dreamstime.com: 10; Joe Robbins: 22 (top); Joseph August/
Shutterstock.com: 22 (bottom); Kae Deezign/Shutterstock.com:
6; Kenishirotie/Shutterstock.com: 12 (top); landmarkmedia/
Shutterstock.com: 23 (bottom); mattjeacock/iStock.com: 13
(bottom); NASA: 23 (center); National Archives:18; Orhan Cam/
Shutterstock.com: 19 (bottom); PictureLake/iStock.com: 19 (top);
rook76/Shutterstock.com: 20 (top); ruvanboshoff/iStock.com: 23
(top); stephen mulcahey/Shutterstock.com: 20 (middle); Teresa
Kasprzycka/Shutterstock.com: 13 (top); traveler1116/iStock.com:
20 (bottom)

ISBN 9781626873674
LCCN 2014930706

Printed in the United States of America
Mankato, MN
July, 2014
PA02214

## ABOUT THE AUTHOR

K.C. Kelley has written dozens of books for young readers on
everything from sports to nature to history. He was born in
January, loves April because that's when baseball begins, and
loves to take vacations in August!

## ABOUT THE ILLUSTRATOR

Bob Ostrom has been illustrating books for twenty years.
A graduate of the New England School of Art & Design at
Suffolk University, Bob has worked for such companies as
Disney, Nickelodeon, and Cartoon Network. He lives in North
Carolina with his wife and three children.

# Contents

# WELCOME TO JULY!

Fireworks and freedom! That's what we celebrate in July. On July 4, 1776, the United States of America was born. July is also packed with summer fun. Long days, good weather, and fun with your friends. That's a month to celebrate!

**July**

**FACT BOX**

Order: Seventh

Days: 31

## HOW DID JULY GET ITS NAME?

In 45 BCE, the Roman emperor Julius Caesar (SEEZ-er) changed the 10-month calendar into a 12-month calendar. Most of the world used this "Julian" calendar until the 1500s. To honor Caesar's birth month, Rome named the seventh month July.

# THREE COOL THINGS ABOUT JULY

- In Australia, July is the coldest month of the year!
- Cover your ears: U.S. military bases fire a 50-gun salute on July 4. Why 50?
- In July 1971, Congress said 18-year-olds could vote!

## Birthstone

Each month has a stone linked to it. People who have birthdays in that month call it their birthstone. For July, it's the ruby.

# JULY AROUND THE WORLD

Here is the name of this month in other languages.

| | |
|---|---|
| Chinese | Qī yuè |
| Dutch | Juli |
| English | July |
| French | Juillet |
| German | der Juli |
| Italian | Luglio |
| Japanese | Shichigatsu |
| Spanish | Julio |
| Swahili | Julai |

# LUMBERJACK WORLD CHAMPIONSHIPS

Sawing, log-rolling, chopping, and climbing: that's what lumberjacks do. Each July, they battle for the top prize in this annual event. A lumberjack from New Zealand has won All-Around Champion 15 times!

# BIG JULY HOLIDAYS

## Independence Day, July 4

On this day, Americans celebrate the birthday of the United States. We remember when we gained our independence from Great Britain in 1776. People wear red, white, and blue, like the flag. They have picnics, play music, and set off fireworks. They have huge parades and fly the flag of the United States.

## THE HAPPIEST PLACE

Kids around the world should remember this day. On July 17, 1955, Disneyland opened! It's in Anaheim, California. Walt Disney himself was on hand to open the park. There were just five theme "lands" in the park. Today, there are eight. Disney's California Adventure is right next door, too. More than 3.6 million people came in 1955. In 2013, more than 15 million visited!

## Canada Day, July 1

Much like Independence Day in the United Sates, Canadians celebrate the birthday of Canada. This holiday was first called Dominion Day. Canadians celebrate Canada Day just as Americans celebrate the Fourth of July—with parades, fireworks, parties, and concerts that honor their country.

## TENNIS, ANYONE?

It's not a holiday, but it's a tradition! Since 1877, the All-England Tennis Championships have been held, usually ending in July. They are played at courts in Wimbledon, a part of London. The greatest tennis players of all time have played in this **Grand Slam** event. America's Pete Sampras and Switzerland's Roger Federer have each seven won Wimbledon titles. Martina Navratilova of the Czech Republic holds the ladies' record with nine.

9

# FUN JULY DAYS

July has more ways to celebrate than just wearing red, white, and blue! Here are some of the unusual holidays you can enjoy in July:

July 1

International Joke Day

**July 2**

World
UFO Day

**July 12**

Pecan Pie Day

**July 14**

Shark
Awareness Day

July 20

Lollipop Day

July 22

Hammock Day

July 24

Cousins Day

**July 25**

Merry-Go-Round Day

**July 28**

National Milk Chocolate Day

**July 31**

World Park Ranger Day

# JULY WEEKS AND MONTHS

Holidays don't just mean days…you can celebrate for a week, too! You can also have fun all month long. Find out more about these ways to enjoy July!

## JULY WEEKS

National Rabbit Week: This week, rabbit lovers spread the word about these fun pets.

National Zookeeper Week: Animals are the stars at zoos. This week, their helpers are stars, too! Find out more about what zookeepers do at a zoo near you!

# JULY MONTHS

**Family Reunion Month:** Most schools are off, so this is a great month to travel. Many families get together. A reunion is when far-off families meet at one place. What are all the places your family lives?

**National Blueberry Month:** How do you like blueberries? In pancakes? In muffins? Or by themselves? July is a great month for picking them . . . and eating them!

**National Hot Dog Month:** Hot dogs are the perfect picnic food! More hot dogs are eaten in July than in any other month.

**Mango and Melon Month:** Summer is a great time to try these tasty, juicy fruits. You can have them plain or mix them with other food. Try a melon salad! Or make mango jam!

15

# JULY AROUND THE WORLD

Countries around the world celebrate in July. Find these countries on the map. Then read about how people there have fun in July!

**July 25**

**Guanacaste Day, Costa Rica**
In 1824, a part of Nicaragua joined Costa Rica. The part was called Guanacaste!

## NATIONAL DAYS

The United States' Independence Day is July 4. The countries of Burundi, Rwanda, Venezuela, Algeria, Comoros, Argentina, Bahamas, Colombia, Liberia, and Peru all celebrate their Independence Days in July.

**Jan Hus Day, Czech Republic**

July 6

People in this European country remember a priest from the 1400s who is a symbol of Czech freedom.

**Bastille Day, France**

July 14

In 1789, French people fought against their king. On Bastille Day, they stormed a famous prison.

**Il Palio, Italy**

July 2

The amazing horse race takes place in Siena, Italy. They race twice each summer. Neighborhoods race against each other. The first Il Palio was in 1656!

**Sea Day, Japan**

THIRD MONDAY

Japan is an island nation. On this holiday, also called Marine Day, they celebrate the waters that surround them.

17

# JULY IN HISTORY

ZIP codes were used for the first time.

President Lyndon B. Johnson signed the **Civil Rights Act**. This helped end many racist laws in the United States.

## ONE GIANT STEP

On July 20, 1969, one of the most famous events in history happened. American astronaut Neil Armstrong became the first human being on the moon. He was joined soon after by Buzz Aldrin. More than half a billion people watched the men. They were part of the American *Apollo 11* space flight.

## July 6, 1933

The first Major League Baseball All-Star Game was played. Babe Ruth hit a home run!

## July 13, 1985

The international concert Live Aid raised more than $250 million to help starving people in Africa.

## July 16, 1790

Washington D.C. became America's capital city.

## July 22, 1620

People known as Pilgrims left England. They arrived in America in November.

## July 25, 1984

Svetlana Savitskaya of Russia became the first woman to walk in space!

## July 28, 1914

World War I began in Europe.

## July 29, 1588

A huge **fleet** of British ships stopped a Spanish invasion. Sir Francis Drake led England to this famous victory.

# NEW STATES!

Three states first joined the United States in July. Do you live in any of these? If you do, then make sure and say, "Happy Birthday!" to your state.

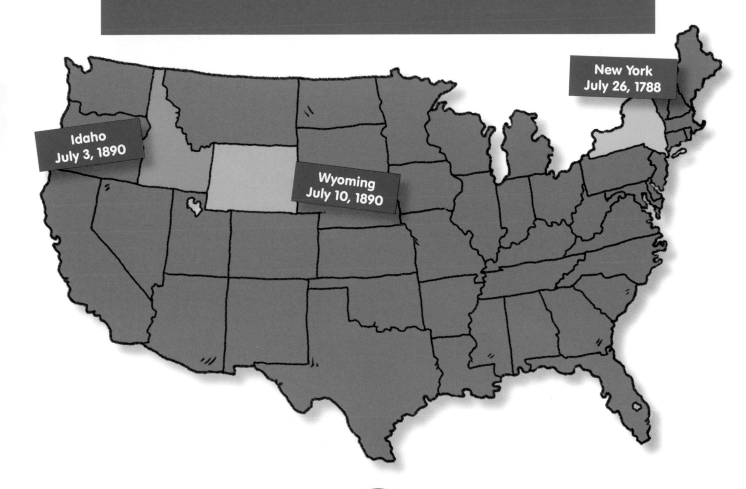

New York
July 26, 1788

Idaho
July 3, 1890

Wyoming
July 10, 1890

# FAMOUS JULY BIRTHDAYS

## July 2

**Richard Petty**
The NASCAR racer known as "The King" won a record 200 races. He was the champion seven times.

## July 5

**P. T. Barnum**
A great 1800s showman, he started a famous circus.

## July 6

**George W. Bush**
He was president from 2001–2009.

## July 16

**Roald Amundsen**
This Norwegian explorer was the first to reach the South Pole.

## July 18

**Nelson Mandela**
This great and courageous leader helped create a free South Africa.

## July 24

**Amelia Earhart**
America's greatest female pilot was the first woman to fly across the Atlantic.

## July 31

**J. K. Rowling**
The Harry Potter author used her birthday as Harry's birthday, too!

# GLOSSARY

**Civil Rights Act** (SIV-il RYTS AKT) This law, signed in 1964, outlawed unequal and unfair treatment of people based on their race.

**emperor** (EM-pur-ur) A person who leads an empire, which is a nation that has taken over other nations.

**fleet** (FLEET) A large group of ships, usually in a navy.

**Grand Slam** (GRAND SLAM) The four major tennis championships held each year: Australian Open, French Open, Wimbledon, and the U.S. Open.

**reunion** (ree-YOON-yun) A gathering of people, usually a family, who have known each other for a long time.

# INDEX